Letters to No One

Written by:

Donald Thompson II

Letters to No One

Copyright © 2019 Donald Thompson II

All Rights Reserved

No part of this publication may be reproduced, distributed or transmitted in any form or by any means, including photocopying recording, or other electronic or mechanical methods, without prior written permission of the author, except in the case of brief quotations embodied in critical reviews and certain other noncommercial uses permitted by copyright law. For permission requests, write to the publisher at the address below.

ISBN: 978-0-99983676-2-0 (paperback)

Library of Congress Control Number: 2019916068

Cover Created by Quay Weston, Enoch Collation

Photograph (backcover) captured by Reko Daye, Suave Visions, LLC

With a Capital M Publishing Group, LLC

P.O. Box 52656

Durham, NC 27717

www.withacapitalm.com

withacapitalm@gmail.com

Special discounts are available on quantity purchases by corporations, associations, and others. For details, contact the publisher at the address above.

Dear No One,

I'm tired of looking for you. So, I'm writing this hoping it will bring you to me...

The Letter Box

Dear Best Friend

To My (K)night

To Anonymous "Because you love Love and I just knew you would be married by now"

Dear No One

To the Reason Why They Tell Me I Can Do Better

To "The One"

My Mother said…

Just End It

To My Fantasy

To Love

To My Enchantress

To Negativity

The Lioness in the Green Dress

To the Perfect One…

To My Words…

Letter to M.E.

To Selflessness

From Temptation

To the Bed that Holds Me Captive

So, I Need a Friend

To Whom it May Concern…

XIIX

Dream Catcher

The Walk (to the restless)

To ….

To the BBT Cousins

To My Distraction(s)

To My Forever…

Amorous ?'s

A Brief Moment of Clarity

From My Enlightened Self

To Grandma

To the Inspiring Alchemist

Play Fair (Alive)

To True Love

To the Oasis

The Note from "The Date"...

Break it Down, Build Your Man

She wants a …

Man of GOD who readily and regularly attends church.

She needs a…

Reader of the word, one willing to kneel and pray.

He needs to…

Be that chivalrous old school man, a door opener if you will

to fulfill her needs…

He needs a job, a car, and yes, a home.

She wants a…

Self-sufficient man whose mind doesn't roam.

She needs him to…

No, he must… love to laugh for

Laughter helps heal the soul;

Especially after the adventures he takes her on

And the great conservations that may lead to songs.

Character may maketh the man but great character maketh hers.

Handsome is his eternal garment of appearance

And royalty, his internal mission.

For his queen is his heart and his love for both has no intermission

She needs a knight not only in spirit but in sport.

Muscles of love pushing left in front of right, right in front of left

As she strolls along the beach of life with him directly beside.

Is he demanding?

No.

Reprimanding?

No One

No.

Understanding?

Yes!

And what scintillating, mentally stimulating
female wouldn't want her man

To enjoy, to want, to love hugging her?

Be an increasing intellectual

While all the same forgiving. A sensual passionate kisser;

that chivalrous old school man,

elegantly, inscribing, enticing letters

of appreciation, elation, inhuman infatuation;

words illustrated through actions of trust and loyalty.

Sweet, nightly, omnipotent prayers for her

with warm, cuddling, fire-lit nights reading by the couch,

date nights less so in, more so out.

The Bruce to her Selina, to her Talia,

An undying bond, a true trust, a best friend

An unconditional, never-ending, ever-giving love;

Keeping her smiling even from the heavens above.

"You can't put everything down," she says

But not knowing to whom she spoke to

And me, full heartedly agreeing...

I had to reply

"There are some things that can never be written in words and that's that!"

By

Love's Rhyme

Chocolate Habanero

You probably don't remember a brother

But every word, every curve, every cold shoulder you served

Is etched in my mind for all time.

What even a son's mother would break down and call a dime

Was how I described you.

Smooth to the touch as we glided across the floor.

Your body in my arms like that red clutch was in yours.

I wanted to give you the exclusive private tour

But you pulled a Cinderella and said you couldn't dance anymore.

No One

You left a brother hanging, almost thirsty, hungry for more.

So, you called, you texted, you threw a little game

And I didn't even know it was just to play with my head, and create more shame…

A Habanero encased in chocolate!

Sweet at first taste, unsuspecting at first glance,

Then when I finally get a chance to chew, to enjoy

You scorched my heart, made me sweat, and brought pain to my joy….

To the ONE

So, I hope you didn't find me offensive or lazy or anything else negative.

I just want you to understand that I have been searching hard and long,

Just to be able to ask you "Can I be your man?"

And, to think that I still don't even know your name…

I don't know if I have heard your voice

And I know this isn't by your choice

But I am starting to lose hope on making it to you.

I'm not sure if I have enough love to give to you.

I want to be the man that does it all, that makes you want to brag about me night and day to your bestie.

But then-you save all the good secret tidbits for your private mind's audience to smile at later.

I want to be the father to our legacy and give you memories of watching me strengthen and protect the lives you brought into this world.

I want to hold you so tight but ever so gently when you needed me most and let your spirit coast to sleep.

Then when it came time to go in deep...

Well you know what you want, I just want to give it to you, be it for you.

And I'm trying to tell you and warn you now that if I can't find you soon...

I don't know what will be left of me.

The world is cruel, it is unrelenting, castigating every fiber of my morality as I desperately attempt to positively pursue prosperity.

The new generation of this earth my task to mentally prepare but my mentality dives to the depths of Joker and Quinn just to maintain a *foothold within true sanity. I don't know how to do it.*

I have prayed for you, I wished for you, I almost thought of even googling for you…

But Siri and Cortana were of no help. So, I just moved on past Tinder and threw my heart's endeavor in cupid's blender.

So, now you probably have an idea of my low but I know if you can just help me get to you, I still have enough to make US truly glow.

No, wait… wrong word, not glow, grow! There we go, I want US to grow together, love together, be together but in more than just heart, soul, and physical reality. I want a spiritual connection with you that cannot be torn, stripped, cut, nor clipped.

I want to feel your pain even if I am worlds away. So, I know to get to you and make your day!

I…

21 Inquiries of the Soul

1. *What seven words/traits describe you?*
2. *Of those seven, which are the four you can do without?*
3. *Of the three words left, which two go well together?*
4. *Do you understand why the word that is left over reflects your individuality?*
5. *What is the purpose of your spirituality?*
6. *What do you care for most your emotional, your mental, your physical, or your sensual being?*
7. *Are you focused on truly answering these questions or are you waiting for a question you aren't scared to answer?*
8. *Who do you see when you look in the mirror?*
9. *When is the best time to be you?*

10. *Why have you decided to give up on love?*
11. *What do you truly want?*
12. *What do you already have?*
13. *What is the one thing you are afraid of losing?*
14. *Where are you scared of going/ending up?*
15. *What are you willing to sacrifice?*
16. *When?*
17. *Where?*
18. *Why?*
19. *What were the three questions that popped into your head for 16, 17, and 18? (because I didn't actually ask you anything)*
20. *Do you think I am playing a mind game with you or have you truly seen the purpose behind these questions?*
21. *What is question 21 supposed to ask? Does it matter? Did you answer the other 20? Were you true to yourself? Did you really count to see if there were actually 21 questions (because I did)? What do you think of me for doing this?*

To the Artist…

As my fingers act like a quill to parchment,

My love will be the ink for my thoughts; I will
Paint with the color scheme of amity.

But I want more than just a cordial
relationship with you.

I don't need cooperation, I crave compassion.

I don't need the safe realm of stick figure
clichés

When we can engender images of timeless
passion,

Stitched to the canvas of memory for all to
see…

That-we are the true masterpiece.

No One

I want our happiness to shine like my celestial element

But with our integrity as transparent as the pyramid of the Louvre.

Every past adventure treasured like the true owner of the Taj Mahal.

As I gaze across the stars I wonder if any native of Pluto, Jupiter, or Mars,

Could understand how deeply I feel for you and am willing to do for you?

To the Woman Who Dares to Try…

I'm lacking a lot on the social side of life

No Twitter drama, no Snap Chat strife, no Instagram wife.

I know how to love but have forgotten how to trust.

So, showing me loyalty would definitely be a must!

I'm no stranger to Argument nor to Fuss

But show me the face of Unity.

Introduce me to Purity of Heart, let's be friends with True Love

Because she never falters, and that's what I want.

Since I will give that to you from the very moment we start talking about the altar.

Let me get back on topic before you forget my point, but the gist is hard to miss…

That you need to realize I "love Love"

And if you want to be the one I put above all else

Well…

Come on and try your best

I will let Destiny handle the rest…

To the One I Want…

I want you to love me like at any second, at this very moment you might lose me.

I want you to feel like I am truly an accessory to the murder of your fears

And lock my heart up tight in yours for the full sentence of life.

I want you to feel the joy that rushes from the depths of my soul when I wake to see your face,

When I come home to your loving, your warmth, and your grace.

I want you to watch your man at work as I quantify the meaning of being yours and define the meaning of trust.

I want you to show me that I can never be let down by those fiery Serengeti eyes; that cool cinnamon sugar frame,

And that your love will still shelter, honor and protect the same.

I want you to think of the most spiritual, intellectual, sensually strong being you know...

Then turn to the mirror to see mine.

I want to hold your soul's hand down the walk of life as legacy after generational legacy grows under our care, our love, our wisdom, our passion.

I want the universe to be jealous of our love's unique fashion.

I want your undying passion.

I want to hear you whisper in my ear "come here" so I can extinguish cold from your thighs, warm winter's bite from your arms, and let you snuggle up close free from harm.

No One

I want to hide away in a rainforest café full of exotic wonders, only to prove you are even rarer still.

I want to travel the world with our eternal happiness solidified and on display. So, people crave to come up and say "have you two always been this way? Can our love be as joyful and bright versus dismal and gray?"

I want you to love me because…

I want to tell you I love you but I rather show you…

"I'd rather be a good man than a great king"

But then again, with you they might be the same thing…

To the Lady M

Dear Caramel Macchiato Goddess,

I'm wondering what wondrous wild wishes wander in your marvelous mind

So, I could send satisfyingly sensuous sensations sliding up and down your spine…

Well now that I have your attention, let me do some lost asset prevention.

Take a tempting glance in a mirror at a truly triumphant woman who dares to let Trouble torture her heart.

Allow me to testify against Negativity, for her family has spent significant time in my kingdom without paying a dime.

Misery loves to stay in proximity of my person, perspiring pestering pestilence.

So, I had to call upon Hope and Endurance to take her away.

Then there was Devastation destroying every delightful moment, displacing the dawn with a distressing disastrous day.

So, understand I know what it feels like when the only person who answers a call or text is Solitude.

I too have been disgraced by Deceit and felt it only right to demote Trust and discontinue his position at my side as a faithful advisor.

But do not let Hate hide the Truth from you for Trust is needed now even more but you must allow Trust to harmonize with you.

Take a chance and allow Clarity to cut the confusion of any cute courteous tricks anyone may try to play on you.

Then you can invite Fun, Social, and eventually Love to come over to play; and maybe even stay since they do help pay the rent.

Well, either way, I hope reading this advice was time well spent.

And thanks for letting me write those first two lines to vent… :)

To the Prince

As your King, your Father, and your most devoted Advisor…

I ask you to simply listen, my Son.

The world will not care for you nor your sister, your mother, your love, or your people.

I have yet to find the reason for this unreasonable hate and dislike but to no avail there is no true cause to rectify.

You will have struggles that test every fiber of your soul, begging your spirit to give in or give up but you must remain strong and whole.

The very second you feel like you should give up is the very second you should remind yourself there is nothing to fear and that you will make it through to live another day.

Protect our house while I am out and if I leave this world before my time.

In order to accomplish this, you need to learn to first protect your own being...

Build your mindset on a foundation of peace, strengthen your mind as much as you strengthen your body.

Inherit morals of positivity, respect, and tranquility.

Develop an unshakeable courage, an unmoving spirit, learn to control your heart to never hate but to appreciate life and its true beauty.

Rule the world with respect, firmness, and longevity but never fear.

And take every moment you can to show your feelings to those you hold dear.

But above all my beloved prince, I ask that you live son, make sure that above all else that you live!

To the Princess

This will probably be the hardest conversation I have with you without ever saying a word out loud

But my dear while I am here…

My back is your shield, my heart your helmet, and my spirit and undying love your sword.

For nothing of you shall perish so long as my breath flows through my body

Your purity my priority and I mean more than just your purity of flesh.

Your mind is the doorway to the soul just like your legs hold the key to the gate of life

Therefore, may you guard them both more than even I restlessly guard your mother.

For the loyal, strong, devoted, intellectual love of my life is a temple where no one enters except me during the proper season.

But regardless of the season, I must cleanse my temple daily, burning the stench of wretched ignorance of the world with the incense of vitality and immortal morality.

Enjoy the fruits of just one man not many

For like one who eats too many oranges the body starts to rot from the teeth

The acid becomes too much, so find The Man who has more than the golden touch

But is in touch with himself, the world, and his Maker.

One who you deem worthy of me saying "yes you may take her"

To My Brother(s)

If you could stop fighting me long enough to listen and watch the world for just a second,

You will see your futile scrummage with me is in vain.

For I neither want to nor have a reason to fight you.

I simply want you to understand what I told my prince, that we are under attack.

They want to demolish the males of our race and tarnish the purity of our Queens.

They are mentally and physically raped every second we yell and every time you curse it only silences their voices.

Every time you "win" a bout for new territory or defending your own, our Queens' territory is rampaged, trampled upon, set fire to by the catalyst of your own ignorance to the fact that fighting with our Queens does not bring prosperity and fighting against a brother, one of your own neighboring Kings won't even guarantee survival through the day.

Every time you leave the house thinking of war, she shakes her head in shame knowing full well that you don't know who the true enemy is and while you are gone she is fully exposed to the Truth.

When was the last time your princess said "thank you for helping me" and it was deserved?

What have you done to ensure her safety past the longevity of your life through hers and her family's?

Why are you still attempting to hit me and getting angry at me even as you read this when society, itself, points out that this is our tragic flaw?

We are the greatest when acting in one accord but not even worth the flavorless gum in your mouth once we turn toward each other in spite.

What will your prince inherit? What type of kingdom does he have to gaze upon and reign over?

Will any of his subjects even remain when you, the current King, allow media to demean the Queen, sell the Princess' body, and then you bring in foreigners to do business while sending your own people on a perilous journey to other countries to fight for bread and water?

Eat not of mine hand fellow king until you act as such and learn to listen to your subjects, your Queen, your advisor, who is frail and ill by your own hand, has no want to lecture any longer. Your teacher, Experience, now taking over as you watch Loneliness spread his gospel across your lands. Despair bringing food to every doorstep while Famine reminds your people why you have no right to the crown in your current state.

Awake dear King! Awake! Become like the Sun and shine rays of life down upon those in need. Leave Treachery, Adultery, and Dishonor to their own outside the Kingdom's gates.

By now you probably feel there is too much going on with what you have read, you understand not the metaphors, the personification of Negativity, nor the fact that your Queen is still being attacked as you continue to read this. Your Queen is the key to the world by the way. Her understanding is deeper than her consciousness can fathom but my point to you is to protect your own. To do that you must understand that your own exceeds your direct family, your friends, your people, your kingdom, your Queen. It is the world, your world that is constantly and consistently under attack and choking from the grasp of Desolation while Annihilation has a dagger in its back.

When you see a brother, help a brother, don't kill a brother.

When you see a sister, love and give to a sister, don't forsake and take from a sister.

When you see a mother, thank her, appreciate her, treat her as your own, don't disrespect her for she is as yours.

When you see a father, listen to a father, watch, learn from a father, don't let a father's strength and wisdom die.

When you see a daughter, protect her, empower her, hinder not her progress to the throne nor defile her.

When you see a son, strengthen him, lead him, tell him what you have learned from the mistakes you made and remind him...

Fighting a Brother is only as fruitful as killing oneself...

Thank you for your time...

Dear Time

I need you to pause so I can take you

And write to various people on my mind.

I need the minutes, the seconds, the hours to empower this pen

And begin to express myself.

I need to take these emotions,

These thoughts off the shelf

And share my wisdom and heart…

I want to write to those whom I've fallen too far apart from.

The friends who still love me and understand and know where I'm coming from.

No One

I have a burning issue pressing on my chest

And I know who would relate to it best

But I have to go here, work there, and I still need to figure out what to do with my hair.

I know you don't care because you keep on going

But I really need you to pause so I can take you

And truly show my family how much I am growing.

A picture, a snap, a tweet, isn't enough

And my life is bigger than some random stuff you pack in the trunk of your past.

I gotta lot to do but you are flying by fast!

So, stop running out for me please, for just a little while.

Unwind, check your gears, or better yet just stop your watch.

I have things to say, people who care, and friends who want to be there…

No…

Be here for me,

And you just keep ticking past three, half past 3, now 4!

Now you are telling me I need to go out the door

And to work, you are such a jerk!

Was it really too much for me to ask?

For you to pause just long enough for my cause?

To My Wife…

We'll face whatever lies in front of us.

For even when we run out of rope

We can still keep each other afloat.

I won't panic if you won't

As we climb the ladder of life.

We shall traverse whole new worlds,

Transcend all limitations,

And enjoy experiences most people don't even dare to dream about.

Yes, this is a bit much to fathom, a lot to consume

But we will be travelers of the world and happiness.

Not just time like those trapped in a 4 walled tomb.

Dear Heart

I apologize for hurting you and putting you through the unrequited bs I help other people avoid

I apologize for abusing you, stringing you up and down, walking you like a yo-yo,

tugging on your leash like a dog despite the fact you were trying to pull me in the right direction all along.

I'm sorry for the long nights where my mind relived the moments my life should have never known.

I shouldn't have even more thought of being in a relationship where…

Communication only worked part- time. trust was M.I.A., and Hope for the Future was forever fading. I know on some days I make you heavy with worry and others are filled with butterflies, adrenaline, and good times.

I'm just trying to figure out this life and fill it with bliss.

Dear Best Friend

I remember when…

You told me I was the craziest person you knew; t was a good thing.

I remember we were the goofy stereotypical nerds. You even had the glasses but we said one day we would be on top, looking good.

I must say you told me so and it feels good like it should to just be myself.

I remember when you cried for me and told me I could be better after seeing my life beaten black and blue.

I think that was the last time you brought ice. I just wish I could have done the same for you.

I could have supported your dreams.

I could have listened to your advice, your heart, your pain…

I just hope our friendship can return and flourish once again!

To My (K)night

That night I just knew I could make it

I played cool, faked it but didn't drink anything

Because I knew I had to make it.

Make it back that is.

I told them all that I was fine, I was good

Putting on a hood of denial

A mask of ignorance

And asking Determination to help me on my quest to Sanctuary

But it was all HIM

Because about half -way there my mind decided to swim

My limbs locked and some way, somehow, for some time unknown…

I was gone from this world,

On that all familiar astro-plane of bliss.

Getting sleep I'm sure I needed, not knowing that at this moment

I was accelerating Death, giving birth to Shock, and setting up Misery to rain on my parade all the way back home.

So, HE helped me, HE made a call, without a phone

Just to me, there that night while I was flying all alone

Woke me up just in time to see the Median between Life and Death.

Speed and Time slowed down just enough for me to observe my present situation,

Gain the realization of what Fate was bringing to my door, and take Action for a spin.

If I ever believed in HIM being all that HE is, it was then…

Like a ball, Blu bounced off Death and as the rims slammed

Into the tires,

Blu ran to the other side of the court,

Stopping right at the bench.

I got out, looked up and down the shoulder.

Popped the trunk and figured out which useless black boulder

Was best to switch out to finish this game of life HE just reset for me.

I didn't know where I was, Shock was choking me.

Gratitude was hitting me.

And all the blessings of life were reviving me to a sound mind.

I thought seeking Sanctuary was a lost cause at that very second

And started wondering about who could help me

Who would be willing to save me?

I had put on a front with those I left so I couldn't ask them.

I had a flower from life's garden close by but there were too many thorns on that stem.

So, I called you,

you answered,

you cared,

You shared enough of your life and time

To remind me my spirit was still here,

That I was human,

That I was still alive,

(I probably should have but...) That I didn't die.

And that night you were my Knight.

No One

You saved me from my plight

And I won't forget

You have my thanks

But know I won't forget…

To Anonymous "Because you love Love and I just knew you would be married by now"

No not me, not yet, maybe eventually

But does Eventually ever show at Today's door?

I mean really?

It's almost been 3 years, nope lol, almost 4

Since that talk and it was about the same amount of time before…

Before that walk, the cry, the pain, the tears,

It was a long drive down the road to picking myself up.

I didn't have the resources to help you do the same.

But I know you are back, no past that now

You can smile, you can love…

You can live

So, I'm moving on to do the same.

Letting go of Shame, leaving Hate

Taking Prosperity on a date

Hopefully, you can relate to the emotional eustress

Life has brought as my worries come to a rest…

Dear No One

I'm tired of looking for you.

So, I'm writing this hoping it will bring you to me…

My heels need healing from treading through barren lands of unrequited deserts,

My soul's hands numb to the touch from scaling the mountains of lonely negativity.

Devastation thought she ruled me for a second and Catastrophe wanted me to be her baby daddy;

But I can't father Misery nor will Seclusion be my spawn.

My legacy is only yours to produce and I hope you come soon.

No One

So, I can relearn my amorous linguistics, I feel like I almost forgot how to caress while cuddling you in your most comfortable position.

I want to be supported with the roots of your smiling nurturing force of proactive contribution,

As I lay the foundation for a family-- known for Success, Endurance, Perseverance, and Loyalty only to Righteousness.

Which brings me back to line one…

I miss you, I need you, I'm waiting for you even now to simply walk in and say "I'm here"

For I'm tired of fighting Fear and Exhaustion as they tag team waiting for Defeat to claim me on his taxes.

As a matter of fact, this crew attacked me just the other day just when I thought you might be coming my way…

Only to realize it was just Denial trying to flirt and so I walked home trying not to show I was hurt.

So, I showered hoping to meet up with Refresh and Rejuvenation but Pain was the only person at my door

And I had tried my best to move on, sit back, relax and ignore her.

With her yelling up and down, wanting me to adore her and say I wanted her to stay

But No, I don't think anyone loves Pain in that type of way.

So, I'm still waiting for you to come my way

And hopefully when you get here, you plan to stay

To the Reason Why They Tell Me I Can Do Better

I dropped my sword to write you a letter

Bought some roses in hopes that we were doing better

But the metaphysics of me trying my best

Seems to come to my loss of breath, my heaviness of chest

Me clenching my breast at the thought of everyone else closer towards clenching your…

Heart

Mind intertwined with Sorrow's memories as friends raise the alarm, pull my legs, and tug at my arms;

Pulling me away from Temptations' devastation.

I keep trying to do better, not realizing the only true issue is finding better, being better for myself

. . .

By not suffering the kamikaze attack of loving you.

To "The One"

I know you haven't found me yet…

But I promise the only thing you will be upset about when you do…

Is that it took this long to find me…

My Mother said…

"One person can only do so much."

But I must be out of touch with reality,

Because I see one person changing the channel to disparity.

Laughing at my people's struggle

As he indulges, makes money, and picks another woman to snuggle under.

The share of power in this world must be unfairly unjust and I wonder

If Evil, Negativity, Negligence, and Ignorance always manage to touch the children

Why can't Knowledge, Prosperity, Wisdom, and Success ever win?

I feel Hope was dropped into an oubliette with Despair and Fear

Overhead watching and laughing to the point of tears.

Still, that line rings in my ears "one person can only do so much."

So how can one person come on a screen and say he can do disrespectfully mean things,

And millions of people agree with his belligerent and filthy morals?

How can one person place so much value on a dollar to the point where generations of his legacy

Only know how to make theirs and take from others even if the other is a blood bound brother?

I fail to understand why someone would use their power to take innocent flowers,

Destroying the trust of our women and eliminating their chance of enjoying the creations their lives were meant to forge.

No One

I watch people create the minds of tomorrow and then one person comes and destroys the dreams of the future with the word "Can't."

Why does it take a village to raise a child but only one person to murder the village?

How can one artist almost eliminate a race, a religion, a group of people?

How can one person face so much hatred just to play the sport he loves?

How can one person hold, love, and care for so many lives only for the world to debate on whether or not to call her a saint?

How can one person's dream outlive himself and still never be reached due to selfishness and arrogant wasteful pride?

How can a father change the dynamics of a family and a community just by staying there for his kid?

I don't know but what I do know is I do all I can

Because…

"one person can only do so much."

Just End It

You are sitting here telling me

That Misery is so consistently inconsistent

It only makes us both sick to our stomach

And I'm patiently waiting for you to treat yourself like a Queen

Once again and get your King of your dreams!

You only give the best of yourself in your work, your projects, your home…

So why let Ignorance leave you standing by the phone?

Why let a Player's lust keep you at home alone,

Stuck in limbo between content and ready to fuss,

When you got your real friends outside looking in ready to fight and cuss?

To My Fantasy

I know you can't be real

But it never gets old, how you make me feel.

Day after day, night and noon

Intoxicated by your earthly scent

Held captive by your…

And your…

I can't wait to spend the time

I can't just date once

I refuse to only see you just once in a dream

With you peeking behind the scenes of my subconscious

Trapped in a world that only makes sense to me when I'm with you

It's a utopia I would normally never escape

except I learned the hard way, a fantasy should stay just that

a fake…

To Love

Heart full, ever lasting

Soul, no longer empty now

Lives to hold, care, share…

To My Enchantress

Time, law, the forces of the universe don't matter,

My infatuation, pure saturation of elation

As my heart indulges, getting fatter,

With every touch, every thought, every memory of our life's' rotation

As each unforgettable day sets into a powerfully soothing night

No city in this world, no word in any language, no song

Can relay the message of the feelings with which you entrap me so tight

And try, as I may with all my might, if what you are doing is wrong, my will to resist is far from strong

Failing to stop the maelstrom of passion thundering its siren songs and flashing its teasing seductions,

Its pouring cascade of kisses down the shorelines of my spine

As the depressions, negativity, and disparity of society are forced into reduction

And my mind can only wrap around your image, my hands around your body, and we intertwine

Because time, law, the forces of the universe don't matter

My infatuation pure saturation of elation

As my heart indulges on the feast, getting fatter

With every touch, every thought, every memory of our life's' rotation

To Negativity

First and foremost, goodbye

I was too patient and too

Willing to comply with your traps, your evil.

You kept me up late into the hours of the morning.

You gave my heart away to those who care

Nothing of me nor for me.

You held me captive with my mouth shut

My eyes open but the lenses could not

Piece through your false disguises...

No more!

The Lioness in the Green Dress

There may be a word that expresses the situation I'm currently in

But I don't care to find it and I'm simply writing this on a whim.

I have a thing for fiery eyes, seductive sorceresses, and silver tongues

But you are different. True, you do have those eyes that ignite my soul every time our desert paths cross.

I just wanted to explain to you, I just wanted to mention…

An unmentionable crime, a silent misjudgment, a withholding of pertinent information.

See, I normally experience a degree of elation just by conversing

No One

With the fibers of your very nature

Your soul and being mature

I find every second of every moment with you

Easy to endure and quite rich

So, let me get down to the matter, the cliché gist

To the Perfect One…

So…

A while back you asked me to write about someone

Describe her, illustrate my love for her,

Explain why she matters so much to me

It has taken a while for me to start writing this

Because I had to first ask myself does she already exist?

Could a Perfect One really and currently walk this earth

And did I meet her, do I know her?

All I ever needed in life was support and a constant reminder

That no matter what I wanted in life I could accomplish.

I need a touch that can soothe pain

A mind that understands limits are a fallacy and

Romance is a two-way street where only true couples converge

While others drive by looking for Fantasy St. or Wish Lane.

I want every (sleep/slumber) to start on a positive note

With no wrath, no jealousy, no hunger for revenge.

Just a peaceful . . . with a hint of . . .

In this era its hard for a man to wear his love on his skin

But I know with her it would be easy, it would be welcome, and I would never have to worry

To My Words…

When I really need you, you fail me

You escape me

You are futile at helping me relate to her.

To she who could possibly use her own words to bring me in to her world…

But no, you fail me

You remain unsaid, undead for when I need you

The conception of your illustrations, your metaphors remain undone.

I normally can use you to have fun and paint a world everyone wants

But now, you are used against me in teases and taunts.

No One

A fight against myself I never asked, never cared for, didn't want.

Why did you let her pass by without a "good day" or "hi"?

Why did you let the one who becomes my soul, fuels my heart leave without a "I will miss you" or "bye?"

So, here is thanks to nothing, to a despair and loneliness emptier than the abyss itself.

Cast down by the syllables that should have lifted me up.

Shattered by the letters and phonics that could not be pronounced.

Now ain't that ironic?!

Letter to M.E.

So…

Hey kid its M.E.

I just wanted you to know how things are turning out.

More people are waking up and starting to see, feel, and shout

The injustices delivered to their doorstep every day

As every night more and more children lay sleeplessly in bed

With sexting on their screens and Hatred killing their dreams

Politicians behind the scenes pushing agendas and

Trying to transcend us common folk

While hoping no one notices their hypocritical lies

Binding the feeble minds of ignorant social followers.

The nation of US is still bullying the rest of the world

Making sure they strike first and worst of all

While prospective presidents want to build walls

To protect their precious silver spoons and racist humiliating cartoons.

Meanwhile you still beat the Sun up and spend the day

Caring more for children then they truly care for themselves

You educate, regulate, dedicate your time

Towards getting children to find their rhyme to Success

Introducing them to Struggle but making sure they get to know Progress.

You show just a few of the infinite possibilities to eliminate Negativity.

No One

Some females still don't treat themselves as Queens

And a lot more just want a money man to keep them.

The men are no better tainting the innocent paintings of their images to the world

And thinking no more of them than hair, eyes, thrills, and curves.

My dear Sir, I must inform you that you try your hardest to prevent these faults

And keep the good with the blessings of those that taught you better

But its not easy,

it takes your all,

it takes a bunch of falls,

Just remember Evil will always press against you

So, stand back up every time.

Regardless of the life you breathe into others

Murderers and thieves will still commit crimes

So, allow Justice to continue to shine.

Above all remain who you are,

Don't change it up for no one

But grow to be better than yourself!

~with love,

Your Older Self

To Selflessness

Talking to this Lady looking real grim

I brought up an unforgiving concept off a whim

Soulmates having to be almost worlds apart

In order to stay alive and protect the other's heart.

A gentleman's nightmare, a true love's curse.

But we both agreed we would do what it took--
for better or worse.

And she specifically said "Selflessness is the purest love."

So, to you, Selflessness I write this prose

For you and only you truly know,

The meaning behind the self-wrenching sacrifices;

Inflicting paradoxical intimate torment,

As a man lives through Pain, only so his one love can live with spiritual, emotional, and mental gain.

Giving continuously, consistently, and eternally for as long as there is power to give, strength to live, and air to breathe.

Has even such a love truly ever been conceived?

I've seen Fathers ran over by social injustices to protect their sons.

Daughters' Mothers screaming their shields of protection against a negative discriminating nation.

Teachers adopting the forsaken children, life has yet to uplift.

But to see the man of virtue, wielding weapons of chivalry, prosperity, and security to love, cherish and uphold…

vows now taken as a meaningless ritual of an unnecessary tradition

It is purely breathtaking.

From Temptation

She said without haste…

My time I shouldn't waste.

That I needed to come over, pull her under…

And have a taste…

A taste of what I've been missing Monday – Thursday

This was Monday so, I'm contemplating, trying not to be a berating

Piece of trash

Like so many other ignorant males chasing as$.

But what to do?

To the Bed that Holds Me Captive

Why do you constantly contain me as the creation of a new day commences, ceasing the nightly transition from the last?

Frustratingly flustering my future plans and fastening my will

Regardless of the season its always perfect

Ready to perform

Resets any defects or deviations to my norm

And therefore I can't let it go

Its my groove, my comfort, my flow

You don't judge, you don't complain

You stay warm and dry, even in the cold and rain

No One

You ease my pain, you dry my tears

You never leave and you always listen with open ears

Night or day you are there for whatever I need

When an old friend leaves

When I just want to read.

So, I Need a Friend

LR- So, I need a friend.

Macchi- "What type of friend?"

LR- One that won't bend towards temptation.

One not afraid to embrace elation despite life's hardships.

Yeah, I need a friendship.

Not a big ship, not a cruise ship

Just an unsinkable ship that won't fall like the titanic

Because my hopes and dreams remain gigantic

And I can't have a friend that easily faints.

Yeah, I need a friend that can help paint the colors of success over our lives

Macchi- Ironically, I was just thinking the same.

Real friends seem to come a dime a dozen.

One-way streets and dead ends have a mirror, the acquaintances I've met over the years.

What I ask for is simple.

Hold me accountable,

Don't agree to my every decision

Let your words reach GOD's ear about me,

And I'll reciprocate

LR- I will hold you accountable if and only if you remember I am reliable,

You must understand that my hands are made to fix

My heart designed to love

My ears tuned to listen

My voice relayed to comfort all despair

As my eyes gaze upon the blessings of this earth

And my mind replays the blessings of those people still here for me

I fall to the floor and express my thanks

I rise to nurture the power, to give back the support

I uplift the Queens and Kings around me

So that models exist for these unhinged princes and disassembled princesses

I just need a friend that understands this world needs a helping hand

I just need a friend who is willing to wake up and share their blessing of life

I just need a friend like you who will be all she can possibly and positively be.

Macchi- Your genuine spirit is what makes this interaction so easy.

Responding to your life's calling takes a trust that only God could give.

See, with my pen I write stories that mend broken hearts,

Create stanzas that create images of succeeding in a dark and dismal place.

Vulnerable, I am on purpose.

I pour out my soul to water the children in my community.

Share laughs with my elders, to renew their falling spirits.

Empathy follows me.

It is in my smile, my touch.

It is in the way that I love.

Compassion is my middle name.

I feel so deep

That others have no choice but to feel their suppressed memories…

I'm here to rebuild, refill, and rejoice in all of my ways.

Faint hearts and closed minds will never stand to the challenge.

But something tells me otherwise about you.

I have one question…

[both in unison] - will you be my friend?

To Whom it May Concern…

A love so bright,

That try as they might,

No one could stare with the naked eye.

A rare phenomenon to behold in the sky of assimilation.

Once in a lifetime elation,

Having you facing your demons of infatuation, impatience and pride.

For you have long since allowed the rays of your heavenly gifts

To be ebbed away by the silhouette of spiritual anarchy.

She already said it…

Your spirit is churning;

Yearning for you to light the match.

To keep the old shit of Yesterday burning

Allowing the winds of Change to blow away the ashes of the Past

Sew your seed of Vitality today.

Water your buds of Prosperity to blossom in its due season

And stop waiting for somebody else's reason

To do, your due diligence

There is a reason why Time only allows Darkness to reign.

Trials are temporary,

Pain is short-lived,

Trouble, Disparity, Inequality are all damaged souls serving a lifelong sentence

Where only you can see them for visitation.

So, stop hesitating at their table, answering their collect calls

And move on down to that dark hall.

The room of your world you left locked, sealed shut

Hurry before it's too late

Find the key

Turn the handle

Feel the strength and rejuvenation,

As Light Rises

Erasing the darkness within.

Saving all.

A Spirit yearning for salvation.

A spirit remembering hope.

A spirit wrapped in the cloth of an unbreakable promise.

A spirit rededicated to true life.

A spirit once again filled with…

Love

XIIX

It's that one day of year

That I hold dearer than dear,

And no, it doesn't belong to me.

andIt probably never will.

But it is also a sad day,

For it reminds me life doesn't always go my way.

But On this day,

A bridge rises from the oceans of despair

And I get to see if everything is ok and fair.

I don't cry anymore,

I don't lay down or fall.

I stand, I speak, I ask, and as always, I actively, lovingly, listen;

As I remember the eyes, the smile, the glisten, the glow of purity.

The strength of an unfailing heart

I'm just glad joy reaches despite my love's grip.

Now, that we are apart

But it's still a day and I must say the meaning behind it

Is just as grand as ever

And you still are a L.A. now, today, and forever

Dream Catcher

Hey you! I miss you and I know you know this is written to you and for you.

So, I hope you don't cry, sigh, or try to remember when & why you said goodbye.

But I just wanted to let you know that you were right!

Before you gave it to me I would sometimes (since my child years) wake up holding my covers extra tight, staring off into the abyss of the night.

Sometimes I had reoccurring frights, other times it was just my fate for watching scary flicks before letting my mind's slumber take flight.

Then you came, you cared, and you shared that mystic item with me and informed me of how love for another powers it and fear cowers before it.

No One

So, I trusted you just like I still do now and hung it up where it still is even now…

I can see it's silhouette now as I write this letter and bittersweetly smile as I recall how I used to sleep better…

Yes, unfortunately I am writing you to ask you if you have forgotten me and how much I care?

Because it's power seems to have been rendered useless even down to the web, beads, and eagle hair.

So, again have you forgotten about me and how much we cared?

Or did life dare to have you remove the memories of a friend so dear you protected for a number of years unbeknown to yourself.

Were you forced to forget like you were forced to let go?

I don't really know…

I honestly don't really know…

No degree or show or wisdom can help me explain what is happening to me…

To this thing…

The only thing that still provides a physical and emotional connection to you.

You may think I'm immature or rude or selfish or stuck in the past but if you do then I don't think you understand what is happening to me.

I am truly scared for as I type, as I hold back tears and write…

I can see the glimpses of the images that used to haunt me and all it does is acknowledge the fact that you have been away for so long that I don't know if your love is gone…

This thing protected my mind and spirit each night for so many years like the mother of that all famous scar and glasses wearing young narrative man we know.

But you were not a mother figure, your relationship was different but truly just as deep.

No One

I hope you had the pleasure of feeling as protected and loved as this 1234567 of yours you keep.

Or at least kept in your mind's heart and your love's eye

But at last I can't fight the sleep anymore

Again, I hope when you read this you will not cry

But maybe reach out and say hi

And maybe…

Just maybe…

For one more night

Your love can hold back

These terrors and frights…

Good night…

Sincerely yours…

The Walk (to the restless)

It's just perspiration

It's not endurance anymore

The repetition of left in front of right,

Right in front of left,

Is no longer a matter of endurance.

Nor dedication, motivation, elation or escape.

Its just perspiration, kinesiology

For the sake of cardio.

I didn't necessarily want to go out today.

I just didn't feel like being in the way of my own success.

So, I got my lazy posterior up and moving.

Now life is back to syncing and grooving with progress.

But I digress, I'm still walking I guess,

Down a path few seem to even

Look down let alone travel.

I guess 21st Century people can't handle gravel.

But yeah, I'm just walking…

To ....

Well an...

Exceptionally Lovable Living Artist...

I doubt you will ever get to read this

But yet I digress...

Because a talent such as yours my heart has missed

For a soul to express the deepest abyss of her emotions

And calm the tormenting seas of everyone else's oceans

Simply because we relate, we understand, we know

What you bring to the world is real.

Your inspiration has me sleepless pulling a Cinderella

No One

Trying to have my mind come back from

This transcendent plane you brought me to before midnight

But to my fatigued delight its already 12:28

And I hate to reiterate but I relate and that's why

My WiFi is wishing it had a curfew

While my neighbors count the clicks of my keyboard instead of sheep

But I doubt me and Sleep will have an affair tonight

Because my heart is floating on every string of your every note

As my spirit devotes itself to the pursuit of why you are so addicting right now...

An opioid of lyrical fashion incased in a silhouette not necessarily surprising

But definitely far from compromising

And regardless if you read this and don't find it faltering

I hope you never stop expressing you…

To the BBT Cousins

"Together forever never apart

Maybe in distance but never at heart"

More than just words curving down her back

A celestial promise of unity, tranquility of mind

Imprinted on her spine for anyone to see that…

She is not confined to the bonds of geography.

Two friends, laughter echoing beyond end

A love transcending even the family tie of blood

Deeper than the marina trench of genetics these cousins.

Lots of good times, yells, screams, and fussing.

Me outside looking in, I see one not a pair

For they are just that much in sync, that coordinated

Extra-ordinary with everything they say or do.

What happens next with S.T. and P.C. I don't have a clue.

Teaching for them to learn but learning so much myself of them

A new rose for the garden of heaven and this phrase at the stem

"Together forever never apart

Maybe in distance but never at heart"

More than just words curving down her back

A celestial promise of unity, tranquility of mind

Imprinted on her spine for anyone to see that…

True love, family, and friendship is not confined by geography

To My Distraction(s)

I don't have time for inaction anymore

Tired of you taking my time that you don't even "enjoy"

Racing to your throne, leaving my own

Condoned to Negativity and Neglect

Only to have you ridicule my intellect

Rip my spirit apart spec by spec

And show me little, if no respect

Well I don't have nothing left

No, I don't have nothing left for you

My Legend will have to be written

Without your mention

I wish I could have known you would try to cancel out my worth to this world

Because I would have treated you

As the wolf you are

But I get it now, I'm on par

Mana charged

Chi replenished

Your influence finished

And with this prose may your existence diminish

You have no dominion here with me…

Begone!

To My Forever…

Today I woke up with a smile on my face

Not just any ordinary smile for

I am thankful to breathe, live and move

But today I will change your life…

You will be…

My air, my water, my sun, my every step,

My every win will be for US.

There will be many just becauses'

Plenty of why nots!

Lots of Let's try

And don't forget

When you cry, I'm your tissue

Today I woke up with one purpose.

No One

I choose to serve by giving to the angel of my heart

As pure as her Serengeti eyes

Burning the doubt from my soul.

I need you and may we share our lives a whole for a whole.

So, by the time

You read this you would have said yes to all the prosperity

Your being can take.

Your ring will be resting in its rightful place on its Queen.

The rest of the world will have been notified (that) you

Chose to be without stress

To live with one who…

Will love past the strife

Through the pain

So that only the blessings remain.

And HIS glory forever reigns over your life.

So, thank you for giving me the mission

Of making every day as beautiful

As today…

So, you always remember

Why you became my…

Amorous ?'s

I see her mind, spirit and physical

Intertwine with the twins of Chaos & Prosperity.

Waiting for a lover's touch but irritated by society's ever-gazing grasp…

A powerful intellectual, chained by her own silence

Self destructively defiant

And unreliant to her true nature and cause

She never takes time to pause

Time to love herself as much as she loves others

No time is wasted on herself as day in and day out

She ensures her family's security

But ironically, her own is forfeit

At least her emotional security

And spirit's stability for she knows not the warmth

Of Love's reciprocation.

She eternally misses the strength of elation from knowing

Everything will be all right because people near and dear

Will help her fight her plight…

No, I'm afraid there is little hope here for her

Love is all but an enigma

A Brief Moment of Clarity

Because You Needed to Reconnect

Hey!!! #SnapSnap

Look at you, connecting with your prose,

As if embracing an old friend.

Holding up your life's light

High as you write the next

Chapter with your heart's pen.

Your spirit the compass,

Path unwoven in time waiting for your love,

Your faith to stitch a fabric so fine.

Stitch it into a tapestry of your world's

Treasures divine and shout to the world
BEHOLD!

For your life is a gift and such a gift gives gifts to the world

For who has yet to stop growing

From My Enlightened Self

Elevating my mind to a higher plain,

No time for silly fame games.

I must remain grounded in my purpose

So, my spiritual wealth can soar

The ultimate goal…

My endgame you ask?

For each new day to be positively more!

To Grandma

Hey Grandma

I haven't met you and I know he hasn't seen you in a long time

But I just wanted to say thank you all the same

For you to only have a decent decade to ensure your spirit descended

To your youngest descendant as a standard of faith and endurance

I commend you.

The power and strength you possess forever captured in the clear framed picture

A picture worth more than the weight of the generations that followed you in gold.

I don't even know how old you are/would be

I'm just glad he was able to know you before you had to leave

I wanted to tell you that despite the fact he may have been in pain

He has been righteous and courageous in all his days

He been strong, constantly weighing right over wrong

And taking all weight on his shoulders

I see only strength in his spirit

I hear only determination in his words

I feel only the power of growth in his actions

And I understand the gravity me inheriting his dominion

So, it is more than my opinion

When I say you did the best you could and all the same

Your best has brought many gifts to this world

And I thank you

And even though I haven't met you

I love you!

To the Inspiring Alchemist

I must inform you without delay

That to much of your dismay

You already have it!

The stone that all on your same journey seek

You want the power to create something from nothing

Yet you have not tapped into the stones you have within yourself

You have a stone, warm to the touch and forever flowing with life

You can bring joy, peace, happiness, even new life into the world

With just a simple tap of this stone

And as far as the other I cannot condone

No One

Such miniscule use of such a gem

For you have not even scratched the rim

Of the stone within the crown of your temple's flesh

Yet I digress

You probably already knew this…

Play Fair (Alive)

Giip Ivgv
D'r bvddvmb czp znx bho'q gipa
V'n kxpreof has zhz axtp tpipv
Zhz peol aeitx nnea V hiol
Vhb rypk na glbn 2 qzgqt
Aeitx sedop gmvto's pbea l ivgz
Geasx xqhob ftgys'p olea l gksyltzakfa vypp ez zpshof
Tk znu gm zna utmglig zt bltpedepi og
Zmpkzvmd oa vost geasx rvofia uldd ng htthrvreho?
Pbevof oi xlpnvmb gmt b hgzzgt, dtivoit ivgv
Har ept axtp pov tihg te' qmaof.
Oh hiuuit khy qpshob, okz dplea, okz ghic V ln
Xhz tvsia zq pxdhailreho ivol b pkedmvu pbr
D ulos zt gvvpp ztho soa dsxapt ng nx ilghp
Dzp znx asyvrr E uler.
L xvhu un tpbti nx emvy
Has zhz hovw deea oi reoi zt pnipi oz sxdliy.

Vhzs palbkvmft ipa evlvq ng gntipnibkz
F fypr gho'q oohu kkz zt neitgkoi nxtvvc
D'r otvmo zh kleg zn tztq umtsxvmb eghzp zna
Hlgbatv L dvh hiol nx kzs vhz...
Oh, L dvh hiol nx kzo na
V gmo's pbea zt ga ukep znw xvhu un tpbta oi vmzt
V lh im vhiog higi ng nx hiolp imf poitvgmta l hiolt
Mg soa drebvt L dkhntv
Tk znu pnhzic V lddkz vhznov zt pevmr ox vhiogr?
Fho'q zmtsx, L xho'p esv nhti ...

To True Love

Living a refreshing, never-ending, constantly growing moment of the greatest joy

Always a surprise, always a truth, always a sunrise with every rain, always a smile

Some will never understand, some will try to stop it, some will try to take it, some will fake having it, some will see it and seek it for themselves

Til the day when all is understood, I will enjoy the fact that I get to spend each day learning something new about you

To the Oasis

Somewhere between land and sea,

I found my love, my heart, my soul

All of the above and more

As I stared at the majestic kingdom of air

And the beaches' shore

This is nothing short of paradise this world

I have been blessed to behold

A hidden oasis of rest untold

The trees, the gentle breeze,

The waves crashing beneath my knees

I long to be here always

With you to live out all my days…

The Note from "The Date"...

So, I went back to that first night

That went just right.

So, I thought and wrestled and fought

With that note where you left me

With an empty ego and no reason to gloat.

Then I notice in the same drawer untouched,

A few more sheets of the same parchment.

Before I could mentally vent,

I traveled through time,

Relaxed my mind and read your words,

With some romantic spine...

"Thanks for a wonderful evening, I enjoyed

It so much! I loved the food, the dancing and your

Gentle touch. I'm sorry I have to go but I'm a

Busy girl you know. Yet I would like to do this again

For sure.

Yours Truly

Forevermore"

That's what I originally thought it said and nothing less

But there lay four more sheets so my mind digressed…

"P.S.

This was a magnificent evening and I know you told me how you felt about me leaving you heart broken. I just wanted to clarify and help you understand why I left. I needed to work on me, it wasn't you. I love

> *you and I love everything you do for me but I had some things to clean up at that time. I still have a few things to work out. I hope you will be as patient with me now as you were then. So, I can be the woman you see me as and return the love you so effortlessly and selflessly give me every day."*

I'm not going to lie those lines woke me all the way up.

I sat up, refilled my cup and prepared to finish the rest of the page with a more open mind that my woman wasn't leaving but needed something I couldn't think to provide. I just wish she had took time to verbally confide in me but I digressed from Negativity as I continued to read the first page of this lover's addendum.

> *"Nights like this keep the image of what our love can grow into forever burned in my consciousness. I can still feel your touch from our dance. It's just as soft as the moonlight on my skin but warm like the hug of a long lost friend. Then again I guess that*

fits because you are my best friend and I this is why I'm writing…

I need close some doors, that I didn't realize I had left cracked. I don't need your help, I will be fine and I'm not in trouble. I have to do this so you and me can be a full WE.

If everything goes according to plan, I'll send you a little something this December. Until then, just love me and know I love you back."

If you feel the same way I feel right now then you probably don't want to know that there wasn't anything on the other sheets, just dried tears from the emotionally well of the deity of my dreams as she scribed her worries to the parchment I let drop to the floor. As the shock of putting everything together and realizing what I need to do…

www.ingramcontent.com/pod-product-compliance
Lightning Source LLC
Chambersburg PA
CBHW051345040426
42453CB00007B/422
* 9 7 8 0 9 9 8 3 6 7 6 2 0 *